EVERYDAY

PRAYERS
for
Families

DIMENSIONS
FOR LIVING
NASHVILLE

EVERYDAY PRAYERS FOR FAMILIES

Copyright © 1995 by Dimensions for Living

Prayers on pages 85-89 © 1995 by Gilbert Caldwell. Used by permission.

This book is printed on acid-free recycled paper.

ISBN 0-687-015804

95 96 97 98 99 00 01 02 03 04 — 10 9 8 7 6 5 4 3 2 1

MANUFACTURED IN THE UNITED STATES OF AMERICA

Contents

A Breath of Prayer

A breath of prayer in the morning
Means a day of blessing sure—
A breath of prayer in the evening
Means a night of rest secure.

A breath of prayer in our weakness
Means the clasp of a mighty hand—
A breath of prayer when we're lonely
Means someone to understand.

A breath of prayer in rejoicing
Gives joy and added delight,
For they that remember God's goodness
Go singing far into the night.

There's never a year nor a season
That prayer may not bless every hour
And never a soul need be helpless
When linked with God's great power.

Author Unknown

Prayers to Begin the Day

O Lord Jesus Christ, who art the Way, the Truth and the Life, we pray thee suffer us not to stray from thee who art the Way, nor to distrust thee who art the Truth, nor to rest in any other things than thee, who art the Life. Teach us by thy Holy Spirit what to believe, what to do and wherein to take our rest.

Erasmus

1466–1536

My Father, for another night
Of quiet sleep and rest,
For all the joy of morning light,
Your holy name be blest.

Henry William Blake

1821–1877

O Lord, bless our family as we gather before leaving to spend our day apart. Help us all to do our best at whatever we attempt. May each of us return to our home tonight with a grateful heart and a cheerful spirit. In Jesus' name we pray. Amen.

Gracious God, we are ready to begin a new week of work and school. Thank you for the rest we enjoyed during the weekend. May we go to work and school with feelings of hope and anticipation for the week ahead. Bless us throughout the day and bring us safely home in the evening. Amen.

Lord God, this has not been an easy time for our family. May this new day bring us strength to face the difficulties in our lives. Stay close beside each of us throughout the day and may a prayer be always on our lips. We praise you and give thanks to you for all your blessings. Amen.

Make us ever eager, Lord to share the good things that we have. Grant us such a measure of your Spirit that we may find more joy in giving than in getting. Make us ready to give cheerfully without grudging, secretly without praise, and in sincerity without looking for gratitude, for Jesus Christ's sake.

John Hunter

1849–1917

Lord Jesus Christ, who alone art Wisdom,
Thou knowest what is best for us; mercifully
grant that it may happen to us only as is
pleasing to Thee and as seems good in Thy
sight this day; for Thy Name's sake. Amen.

Henry VI

1421–1461

Fill us, we pray, with your light and life that
we may show forth your wondrous glory. Grant
that your love may so fill our lives that we may
count nothing too small to do for you, nothing
too much to give and nothing too hard to bear.

Ignatius of Loyola

1491–1556

Lord, behold our family here assembled. We thank thee for this place in which we dwell; for the love that unites us; for the peace accorded us this day; for the hope with which we expect the morrow; for the health, the work, the food, and the bright skies, that make our lives delightful; for our friends in all parts of the earth, and our friendly helpers . . . Let peace abound in our small company. Purge out of every heart the lurking grudge. Give us grace and strength to forbear and to persevere. Offenders ourselves, give us the grace to accept and to forgive offenders. Forgetful ourselves, help us to bear cheerfully the forgetfulness of others. Give us courage and gaiety and a quiet mind. Spare to us our friends, soften to us our enemies. Bless us, if it may be, in all our innocent endeavors. If it may not, give us the strength to encounter that which is to come, that we be brave in peril, constant in tribulation, temperate in wrath, and in all changes of fortune, and, down to the gates of death, loyal and loving one to another. As the clay to the potter, as the windmill to the wind, as children of their sire, we beseech of thee this help and mercy.

Robert Louis Stevenson

1850–1894

New every morning is the love
Our waking and uprising prove;
Through sleep and darkness safely brought,
Restored to life, and power, and thought.

New mercies, each returning day,
Hover around us while we pray;
New perils past, new sins forgiven,
New thoughts of God, new hopes of heaven.

John Keble

1792–1866

Bless me, and all I am to go about and do this day, with the blessing of thy love and mercy. Continue thy grace and love in Jesus Christ upon me, and give me a mind cheerfully to follow thy leadings and execute thine appointment. Let thy Holy Spirit guide me in my beginning, and my progress, on to my last end.

Jacob Boehme

1575–1624

Living Lord, you have watched over me, and put your hand on my head, during the long, dark hours of night. Your holy angels have protected me from all harm and pain. To you, Lord, I owe life itself. Continue to watch over me and bless me during the hours of day.

Jacob Boehme

1575–1624

Rule over me this day, O God, leading me on the path of righteousness. Put your Word in my mind and your Truth in my heart, that this day I neither think nor feel anything except what is good and honest. Protect me from all lies and falsehood, helping me to discern deception wherever I meet it. Let my eyes always look straight ahead on the road you wish me to tread, that I might not be tempted by any distraction. And make my eyes pure, that no false desire may be awakened within me.

Jacob Boehme

1575–1624

My God, Father and Preserver, who in your goodness has watched over me in this past night and brought me to this day, grant that I may spend the day wholly in your service. Let me not think or say or do a single thing that is not in obedience to your will; but rather let all my actions be directed to your glory and the salvation of my brethren. Let me attempt nothing that is not pleasing to you; but rather let me seek happiness only in your grace and goodness. Grant also, that as I labor for the goods and clothing necessary for this life, I may constantly raise my mind upwards to the heavenly life which you promise to all your children.

John Calvin

1509–1564

Most merciful God, order my day so that I may know what you want me to do, and then help me do it. Let my thoughts frequently turn to you, that I may be obedient to you without complaint, patient without grumbling, cheerful without solemnity. Let me hold you in awe without feeling terrified of you, and let me be an example to others without any trace of pride.

Thomas Aquinas

1225–1274

Prayers in the Evening

Lord, support us all the day long in this troublous life, until the shades lengthen, the evening comes, the busy world is hushed, the fever of life is over, and our work is done. Then, Lord, in your mercy grant us safe lodging, a holy rest, and peace, at last, through Jesus Christ our Lord.

John Henry Newman

1801–1890

Now I lay me down to sleep
I pray Thee, Lord, my soul to keep,
In peace and safety 'till I wake,
And this I ask for Jesus' sake.

Now I lay me down to sleep.
I pray the Lord my soul to keep.
While I live I want to be
From quick and angry thoughts set free.
With gentle thoughts and smiling face
And pleasant words in every place.
I pray, whatever wrong I do,
I may not say what is not true;
Be willing in my task each day,
And always honest in my play.
Make me unselfish with my joys,
And share with other girls and boys;
Kind and helpful to the old
And prompt to do what I am told.
Bless every one that I love, and teach
Me how to help and comfort each.
Give me the strength right living brings,
And make me good in little things. Amen.

Lord, keep us safe this night,
Secure from all our fears;
May angels guard us while we sleep,
Till morning light appears.

John Leland

1754–1841

Glory to thee, my God, this night
For all the blessings of the light;
Keep me, O keep me, King of kings,
Beneath thine own almighty wings.

Forgive me, Lord, for thy dear Son,
The ill that I this day have done,
That with the world, myself and thee
I, ere I sleep, at peace may be.

O may my soul on thee repose,
And with sweet sleep mine eyelids close,
Sleep that may me more vigorous make
To serve my God when I awake.

Thomas Ken

1637–1711

Dear Jesus, as a hen covers her chicks
with her wings to keep them safe, do you
this night protect us under your golden
wings. Amen.

Traditional

India

Into your hands, O Lord, we commend our souls and bodies, beseeching you to keep us this night under your protection and to strengthen us for our service on the morrow, for Christ's sake.

Archbishop Laud

1573–1645

Send your peace into my heart, O Lord, that I may be contented with the mercies of this day and confident of your protection for this night; and having forgiven others, even as you forgive me, may I go to rest in tranquility and trust; through Jesus Christ our Lord. Amen.

St. Francis of Assisi

1182–1226

Watch, dear Lord, with those who wake, or watch, or weep tonight, and give your angels charge over those who sleep; Tend your sick one, O Lord Christ, rest your weary one, bless your dying ones, soothe your suffering ones, pity your afflicted ones, shield your joyous ones, and all for your love's sake. Amen.

St. Augustine

354–430

As I take off my dusty, dirty clothes, let me also be stripped of the sins I have committed this day. I confess, dear Lord, that in so many ways my thoughts and actions have been impure. Now I come before you, naked in body and bare in soul, to be washed clean. Let me rest tonight in your arms, and so may the dreams that pass through my mind be holy. And let me awake tomorrow, strong and eager to serve you.

Jacob Boehme

1575–1624

I thank you, O God, for your care and protection this day, keeping me from physical harm and spiritual corruption. I now place the work of the day into your hands, trusting that you will redeem my errors and turn my achievements to your glory. And I now ask you to work within me, trusting that you will use the hours of rest to create in me a new heart and new soul. Let my mind, which through the day has been directed to my work, through the evening be wholly directed at you.

Jacob Boehme

1575–1624

Prayers at Mealtime

You who give food to all flesh,
who feeds the young ravens that cry unto you
and has nourished us from our youth up;
fill our hearts with good and gladness
and establish our hearts with your grace.

Lancelot Andrewes

1555–1626

Father in heaven, thank you for this food from your good earth. Thank you for our home and our family. Sit with us at the table and guide us in all we think and say and do. Stay with us all through the day. Amen.

Bless us, O Lord, and these thy gifts, which we are about to receive from thy bounty, through Christ our Lord. Amen.

Gracious God, as we come to another meal, we pray that we will not be selfish or greedy or careless with the food you have provided for us. Stop us when we are doing wrong things and show us how to do right things. Keep us from saying or thinking any unkind thoughts. Help us to help others, just as you do. In your son's name. Amen.

Bless us, O Lord,
Bless our food and drink,
You Who has so dearly redeemed us
And has saved us from evil,
As You have given us this share of food,
May You give us our share of the
everlasting glory.

Ancient Irish Blessing

To God who gives our daily bread
A thankful song we raise,
And pray that he who sends us food
May fill our hearts with praise.

Thomas Tallis

1505–1585

O Lord, who is the giver of all good things, fill our hearts with gratitude for the food and drink laid before us. And as we fill our bellies, may we be sober and frugal in our eating, taking only that which is necessary to refresh ourselves for your service. Let the pleasure we take in the bread which nourishes our earthly bodies, be as nothing to the joy we take in the spiritual bread of your truth, which nourishes the soul.

John Calvin

1509–1564

Our gracious Lord, thank you for the tree which brings forth fruit in season, for ripening grain, for meat which gives us strength. Help us to always be mindful of your love which planned all things for your children. Amen.

O Tender Shepherd, you lead us in green pastures by gently flowing streams. By your mercy help us to feed your lambs and offer cooling drinks to the sheep of your flock. Through Jesus Christ. Amen.

Dear God, thank you for your promise: "While the earth remains, seedtime and harvest, cold and heat, summer and winter, day and night will not cease." Amen.

(Genesis 8:22)

As the sun doth daily rise,
brightening all the morning skies,
so to thee with one accord
lift we up our hearts, O Lord.

Day by day provide us food,
for from thee come all things good;
strength unto our souls afford
from thy living bread, O Lord.

> Latin hymn;
> translated by J. Masters;
> adapted by Horatio Nelson, 1864

A Thanksgiving Prayer

Gracious God, you are the giver of all things. Today we give special thanks for all the gifts you have given us—gifts we often take for granted. Today we celebrate the gifts of family, friends, love, and life and say "thank you" for the many ways you have blessed us.

[Each person says a sentence prayer beginning "Thank you, God, for . . .]

For all these things, and the meal before us, we give you thanks, O God. Help us always to have grateful hearts. We pray in Jesus' name—your greatest gift of all. Amen.

A Birthday Prayer

Be with us, O Lord, as we share this meal from your bounty and recall with joy the day _____ was born. You have filled our lives with your blessings. We will praise you forever. Amen.

A circle of friends is a blessed thing.
Sweet is the breaking of bread
   with friends.
For the honor of their presence
   at our board
We are deeply grateful, Lord.

Thanks be to Thee for friendship shared,
Thanks be to Thee for food prepared.
Bless thou the cup; bless thou the bread;
Thy blessing rest upon each head.

Walter Rauschenbusch

1861–1918

Praise to the King of Plenty,
Praise every time to God,
A hundred praises and thanks to Jesus Christ
For what we have eaten and shall eat.

Ancient Irish Blessing

Prayers for Home and Family

O God, make the door of this house wide
    enough
to receive all who need human love and
    fellowship,
and a heavenly Father's care;
and narrow enough to shut out all envy,
    pride and hate.
Make its threshold smooth enough
to be no stumbling block to children or to
    straying feet,
but rugged enough to turn back the
    tempter's power;
make it a gateway to thine eternal
    kingdom.

Thomas Ken

1637–1711

To all else thou hast given us,
O Lord,
we ask for but one thing more:
Give us
grateful hearts.

George Herbert

1593–1633

Let us, with a gladsome mind,
Praise the Lord, for He is kind;
For His mercies still endure,
Ever faithful, ever sure.

All things living
He doth feed,
His full hand supplies their need:

Let us with a gladsome mind
Praise the Lord, for He is kind.

John Milton

1609–1674

Lift up our hearts, we beseech thee, O Christ, above the false show of things, above fear, above laziness, above selfishness and covetousness, above custom and fashion, up to the everlasting truth and order that thou art; so that we may live joyfully and freely, in faithful trust that thou art our Saviour, our example and our friend, in this world and in the world to come.

Charles Kingsley

1819–1875

O Great Spirit
   whose breath gives life to the world,
   and whose voice is heard in the soft breeze;
We need your strength and wisdom.
Cause us to walk in beauty. Give us eyes
   ever to behold the red and purple sunset.
Make us wise so that we may understand
   what you have taught us.
Help us learn the lessons you have hidden
   in every leaf and rock.
Make us always be ready to come to you
   with clean hands and steady eyes,
so when life fades like the fading sunset,
   our spirits may come to you without
      shame.

Native American
Traditional

Help each of us, gracious God,
to live in such magnanimity and restraint
that the Head of the church may never
have cause to say to any one of us,
   "This is my body, broken by you."

From China

The Blessing of God
rest upon all those who have been kind to us,
have cared for us, have worked for us,
    have served us,
and have shared our bread with us at this
    table.

Our merciful God,
reward all of them in your own way.
For yours is the glory and honor forever.
Amen

St. Cyril of the Coptic Orthodox Church

Ca. 412

O God Our Father,
the foundation of all goodness,
Who has been gracious to us,
not only in the year that is past but
throughout all the years of our lives;
we give you thanks for your loving kindness
which has filled our days
and brought us to this time and place.

John Wesley

1703–1791

O eternal God,
  in whose appointment our life stands,
  and who committed our work to us,
  we commit our cares to you.
We thank you that we are your children
  and that you have assured us that,
  while we are intent upon your will,
  you will heed our wants.
Fill us with that compassion for others'
      troubles
  which comes from forgetfulness of our own;
with the charity of those who know their
  own unworthiness;
and with the glad hope of the children of
      eternity.
And to you,
  the Beginning and End, Lord of the living,
  Refuge of the dying,
  be thanks and praise for ever. Amen.

James Martineau

19th Century

May the road rise to meet you,
May the wind be always at your back,
May the sun shine warm upon your face,
The rains fall soft upon your fields and,
Until we meet again,
May God hold you in the palm of his hand.

An Irish Blessing

A Vacation Prayer

Dear Lord, it's time for our family vacation. How long it seems that we have been waiting for it, and now it's finally here! Thank you, Lord, for the opportunity to take a break from our daily routine and to replenish our minds, bodies, and spirits. Help us not to worry about having the "perfect" vacation but to relax and enjoy every moment, whatever it may bring. Make us grateful for the joys that await us—whether they be the beauty of your creation, recreation within our family, or peace and solitude. Watch over us and protect us as we travel, and bring us safely home again. Amen.

When Our Family Quarrels

O gracious God, Father of us all, our family cannot seem to get along just now, and we ask for your guidance. Grant us patience with each other. Help us each Lord, to remain calm, sane, and unruffled. May we turn to others to quiet, to comfort, and to smile. Amen.

For a Busy Day Together

Lord, we are looking forward to a busy day together. Help us to look at the other members of our family and try to catch their enthusiasm. Because our interests are varied, we may not always want to be doing the same thing, but with your help we can spend a pleasant day together and learn more about each other. Give us patience as the day grows longer, as we grow tired, and tempers wear thin. It is our prayer that we will end the day with eagerness to spend another together. Amen.

For Disappointment

Lord, our family has suffered a disappointment. Something we've hoped for, dreamed of, and yes, even prayed for is just not to be. We are hurting, Lord, and we are angry. Help us to turn loose of this bitterness. Just now we can see only darkness and despair. Light your lamp within our home. May we see clearly through this shadow that has fallen across our lives. Remind us that just as the darkness of night only hides the day for a few hours, your light shines on behind the darkness of our disappointments. Amen.

A Daily Prayer

O God, let our family make this our prayer every day. Keep us from thinking any critical thoughts about each other or about those we will meet. Keep us from blaming others for our own faults. Keep us from becoming resentful. Let us not say or think any hurtful things about anyone. Help us today and every day to think good and do good regardless of what others may say or do. Help us to stop worrying and fretting. Help us to stop rebelling against circumstances, and, most of all help us to be like Jesus. Amen.

Give me, dear Lord, a pure heart and a
wise mind, that I may carry out my work
according to your will. Save me from all
false desires, from pride, greed, envy and
anger, and let me accept joyfully every task
you set before me. Let me seek to serve the
poor, the sad and those unable to work.
Help me to discern honestly my own gifts
that I may do the things of which I am
capable, and happily and humbly leave the
rest to others. Above all, remind me
constantly that I have nothing except
what you give me, and can do nothing
except what you enable me to do.

Jacob Boehme

1575–1624

My God, Father and Savior, since you have commanded us to work in order to meet our needs, sanctify our labor that it may bring nourishment to our souls as well as to our bodies. Make us constantly aware that our efforts are worthless unless guided by your light and strengthened by your hand. Make us faithful to the particular tasks for which you have bestowed upon us the necessary gifts, taking from us any envy or jealousy at the vocations of others.

Give us a good heart to supply the needs of the poor, saving us from any desire to exalt ourselves over those who receive our bounty. And if you should call us into greater poverty than we humanly desire, save us from any spirit of defiance or

resentment, but rather let us graciously
and humbly receive the bounty of others.
Above all may every temporal grace be
matched by spiritual grace, that in both
body and soul we may live to your glory.

John Calvin

1509–1564

Lord, give me grace to use this world so as not to abuse it. Lord, grant that I may never go beyond or defraud my brother in any matter; for thou art the avenger of all such.

Thomas Ken

1637–1711

Think often on God, by day, by night, in your business and even in your diversions. He is always near you and with you; leave him not alone.

Brother Lawrence

1611–1691

My God, since You are with me, and since it is Your will that I should apply my mind to these outward things, I pray that you will give me the grace to remain with You and keep company with You.

But so that my work may be better, Lord, work with me; receive my work and possess all my affections. Amen

Brother Lawrence

1611–1691

O God, grant us in all our doubts and uncertainties the grace to ask what you would have us do; that the spirit of wisdom may save us from all false choices, and that in your light we may see light, and in your straight path may not stumble, through Jesus Christ our Lord.

William Bright

1824–1901

O Lord, renew our spirits and draw our hearts unto yourself, that our work may not be to us a burden but a delight; and give us such a mighty love to you as may sweeten our obedience. O let us not serve you with the spirit of bondage as slaves, but with cheerfulness and gladness, delighting in you and rejoicing in your work.

Benjamin Jakes

1647–1724

When many are coming and going and there is little leisure, give us grace, O heavenly Father, to follow the example of our Lord Jesus Christ, who knew neither impatience of spirit nor confusion of work, but in the midst of his labors held communion with you, and even upon earth was still in heaven; where he now reigns with you the Holy Spirit world without end.

C. J. Vaughan

1816–1897

For joys of service, thee we praise,
whose favour crowneth all our days;
For humble tasks that bring delight,
when done, O Lord, as in thy sight.
Accept our offerings, Lord most high,
our work, our purpose sanctify,
and with our gifts may we have place,
now in the Kingdom of thy grace.

St. Venantius

530–609

The belt of Christ about me on my going
out and on my coming in.

Ancient Irish blessing

Teach me, my God and King,
In all things thee to see.
And what I do in any thing,
to do it as for thee.

George Herbert

1593–1632

Prayers for the School Day

For a Child's First Day

Dear God, here is —————, ready for her first day at school. She has been counting the days. She is so thrilled.

Be with her today when she goes into unfamiliar rooms, when she sees new faces (make them kind faces!), when she stands in the lunch line, when she is on the playground. Keep her close to you as she learns and grows and makes friends. Protect her from harm. Watch over her on the way to and from school. And as she becomes part of a larger world, help me to let her go and gain experience that she will need to become a responsible part of your creation. Amen

I implore you, good Jesus, that as in your mercy you have given me to drink in with delight the words of your knowledge, so of your loving kindness you will also grant me one day to come to you, the fountain of all wisdom, and to stand for ever before your face. Amen.

The Venerable Bede

673–735

Almighty God, the fountain of all wisdom: Enlighten by your Holy Spirit those who teach and those who learn, that, rejoicing in the knowledge of your truth, they may worship you and serve you from generation to generation; through Jesus Christ our Lord, who lives and reigns with you and the Holy Spirit, one God, for ever and ever. Amen.

The Book of Common Prayer

O Lord, who is the fountain of all wisdom and learning, you have given me the years of my youth to learn the arts and skills necessary for an honest and holy life. Enlighten my mind, that I may acquire knowledge. Strengthen my memory that I may retain what I have learned. Govern my heart, that I may always be eager and diligent in my studies. And let your Spirit of truth, judgment and prudence guide my understanding, that I may perceive how everything I learn fits into your holy plan for the world.

John Calvin

1509–1564

Almighty God, our heavenly Father, without whose help labor is useless, without whose light search is vain, invigorate my studies, and direct my inquires, that I may, by due diligence and right discernment, establish myself and others to your holy faith. Take not, O Lord, your holy Spirit from me; let not evil thoughts have dominion in my mind. Let me not linger in ignorance, but enlighten and support me, for the sake of Jesus Christ our Lord. Amen.

Samuel Johnson

1709–84

Grant, O Lord, to all students, to love that which is worth loving, to know that which is worth knowing, to praise that which pleaseth thee most, to esteem that which is most precious unto thee, and to dislike whatsoever is evil in thine eyes. Grant that with true judgement they may distinguish things that differ, and, above all, may search out and do what is well-pleasing unto thee; through Jesus Christ our Lord.

Thomas á Kempis

ca. 1380–1471

We implore thy blessing, O God, on all the men and women who teach the children and youth of our nation, for they are the potent friends and helpers of our homes. Into their hands we daily commit the dearest that we have, and as they make our children, so shall future years see them. Grant them an abiding consciousness that they are co-workers with you, great teacher of humanity, and that you have charged them with the holy duty to bring forth from the budding life of the young the mysterious stores of character and ability which you have hidden in them.

Walter Rauschenbusch

1861–1918

In the name of God who made a pathway of
the waves,
May He bring us safely home at the end of
the day.

Ancient Irish Blessing

Be thou a bright flame before me,
Be thou a guiding star above me,
Be thou a smooth path below me,
Be thou a kindly shepherd behind me,
Today—tonight—and forever.

St. Columba of Iona

521–597

God's Aid

God to enfold me,
   God to surround me.
God in my speaking,
   God in my thinking.

God in my sleeping,
   God in my waking,
God in my watching,
   God in my hoping.

God in my life,
   God in my lips,
God in my soul,
   God in my heart.

God in my suffering,
   God in my slumber,
God in mine ever-living soul,
   God in mine eternity.

Ancient Celtic

Dealing with Death

God, we never accept willingly the death of someone who is close to us, even though we know that death is a reality for all of us. Help us, in the midst of our grief, with its pain and anger and deep sense of loss, to experience your love and concern that is present, always. Amen

Gilbert H. Caldwell

20th century

In Sickness

God, I have discovered that when I am sick, I talk to you in a different way. I ask you for strength, I ask you, why? I seek your healing comfort. Even though my health problem is inconvenient, let me, with your help, use my moments of treatment and recovery to learn more about you, those whom I love, and about myself. Amen.

Gilbert H. Caldwell

20th century

For Strength to Change

God, other people have told me many, many times that I sometimes have an "attitude", that makes me difficult to take. I know that when I am angry and defensive and insecure, I do things that are not always helpful and healthy. God, help me to confront myself, and when I have done that, give me the will and the strength to change. Amen.

Gilbert H. Caldwell

20th century

Accepting the Fact That I Am Old

God, there was a time when I would laugh at "old people," with their ancient attitudes and crankiness. Now, God, I have to face the fact that *I* am old. Lord, I have discovered that to be able to admit that I am old is liberating! In fact, it can bring a smile to my face and my spirit. Sure there are some things that I cannot do as quickly as I used to, but I have the joy of still being here, and I have the opportunity to share with, and mentor, and watch, younger people as they, too, grow old. Thanks, God, for helping me to accept with joy who I am. Amen.

Gilbert H. Caldwell

20th century

For Those with AIDS

God, we have allowed our practice of Christianity to sometimes express itself in denial, avoidance and self-righteousness. Help us, Lord, to break free of our fear, for it is not worthy of you. Many of us are hurting because we do not know how to handle our illness or the illness of someone close to us. Help us to be the kinds of persons and community that love and care, rather than despise and reject. Amen.

Gilbert H. Caldwell

20th century

Jesu, since thou me made and bought,
Thou be my love and all my thought,
And help that I may to thee be brought;
Without thee I may do naught.

Jesu, since thou must do thy will,
And nothing is that thee forbid;
With thy grace my heart fulfill,
My love and my liking in thee set.

Jesu, at thy will
I pray that I might be;
All my heart fulfill
With perfect love to thee.

That I have done ill,
Jesu, forgive thou me;
And suffer me never to perish,
Jesu, for pity. Amen.

Richard Rolle
(adapted)
1290–1349

As plentiful as the grass that grows,
   Or the sand on the shore,
      Or the dew on the lea,
   So be the blessings of the King of Grace
On every soul that was, that is, or will be.

Ancient Irish Blessing

Christmas

Help us, Lord, to find gladness in our hearts because the light of divine love came down at Christmas time and became a light that will never go out. No sadness can rob us of its joy, no sorrow can take it away. We find cheer at this season in our family circle when we mean more to each other, and when we try to stop time and hold these fleeting minutes. Bless us this year as we gather together and as our love glows with your love in our hearts.

New Year's Day

O gracious God, we praise your name for you never change. As the new year begins, help us to find pleasure in the changes that will occur. As we pray for your blessings in the year to come, we offer our thanksgiving for all your blessings in the year past.

Easter

O eternal One, we praise you for your gift of your son Jesus Christ, our Lord. We remember his passion and sacrifice for sinful humanity, we remember his death and we celebrate his resurrection. Thank you for your promise of eternal life for all your children.